POEMS FROM THE PLAYGROUND

Edited By Wendy Laws

First published in Great Britain in 2023 by:

Young Writers
Remus House
Coltsfoot Drive
Peterborough
PE2 9BF
Telephone: 01733 890066
Website: www.youngwriters.co.uk

All Rights Reserved
Book Design by Ashley Janson
© Copyright Contributors 2023
Softback ISBN 978-1-80459-999-0

Printed and bound in the UK by BookPrintingUK
Website: www.bookprintinguk.com
YB0570B

FOREWORD

For Young Writers' latest competition This Is Me, we asked primary school pupils to look inside themselves, to think about what makes them unique, and then write a poem about it! They rose to the challenge magnificently and the result is this fantastic collection of poems in a variety of poetic styles.

Here at Young Writers our aim is to encourage creativity in children and to inspire a love of the written word, so it's great to get such an amazing response, with some absolutely fantastic poems. It's important for children to focus on and celebrate themselves and this competition allowed them to write freely and honestly, celebrating what makes them great, expressing their hopes and fears, or simply writing about their favourite things. This Is Me gave them the power of words. The result is a collection of inspirational and moving poems that also showcase their creativity and writing ability.

I'd like to congratulate all the young poets in this anthology, I hope this inspires them to continue with their creative writing.

CONTENTS

Appleton Wiske CP School, Appleton Wiske

Zak Sanerivi (9)	1
Grace Bell (9)	2
Beatrix Dyke (11)	3
Annabelle Race (9)	4
Dylan Bateson (8)	5
Bella Sygrove (7)	6
Maddy Turner (8)	7
William Ferrie (8)	8
Noah Saye (9)	9
Lily Easby (10)	10
Barney Rickard (7)	11
Arthur Turner (7)	12

Ennerdale CE Primary School, Ennerdale Bridge

Olivia Hyland (10)	13
Rose Christie (10)	14
Adara Park (10)	15
Charlotte Messenger (10)	16
Iris Benn (10)	17
Luke Walker (10)	18
Matilda Young (9)	19
Emilia Johns (10)	20
Artie Sisson (9)	21
Nieve Fye	22
Joshua Tandy (9)	23
Max Ridehalgh (9)	24
Dylan Richardson (8)	25
Arabella Carr (8)	26
Emmeline Ditchburn (8)	27
Ollie Walker (8)	28
Eva Steel (9)	29

Gabriella Johns (8)	30
Zac Messenger (7)	31
Bridget Christie (7)	32
Chloe Fye (7)	33
Eleanor Riley (8)	34

Eyke CE Primary School, Woodbridge

Sebastian Henderson-Holmes (8)	35
Dexter Lawrence (8)	36
Albert Potter (8)	37
Alice Magill (7)	38
Cayden Allsopp (7)	39
Evie-Rose Mayhew (7)	40
Rafe Fisher (7)	41
Amelie Dorman (8)	42
Georgia Clouting (8)	43
Alex Dobing (7)	44
Morris Hambling-Jones (7)	45
Penelope Waites (8)	46
Ralph Williams (8)	47
Lucas Turner (7)	48
Theodore Burnett (7)	49
James Ahlschlager (7)	50
Rose Henderson (7)	51
Chloe Fortier (7)	52

St Elphin's (Fairfield) CE (VA) Primary School, Warrington

Ruben Livett (10)	53
Molly Finchett (10)	54
Nikola Rusev (11)	56
Sharvani Kahane (11)	57

Favorine Rajasingh (11)	58	Melissza Puskas (9)	101
Harrison O'Keefe (10)	59	Sadie Leigh (7)	102
Tilly-Grace Carter (10)	60	Mohammad Abdan Ullah (9)	103
Harry Stewart (10)	61	Zoya Khan (7)	104
Bethany McAleese (10)	62	Safaa Ali (7)	105
Prithviraj Chauhan (10)	63	Imogen Hartley (7)	106
Ana Popesu (10)	64	Daisy Hartley (7)	107
Ivy Valade (10)	65	Narges Malek Zadeh (10)	108
Scarlett Smith (11)	66	Imaan Asim (7)	109
Macie Lea (11)	67	Noor-Fatima Shah (9)	110
Alexis Hatchman (10)	68	Armaan Khan (9)	111
Oscar Burgess (10)	69	Mason Alan Barry Hanlon (9)	112
Ellie Brown (11)	70	Raza Mohammed (10)	113
Luca Harrison (10)	71	Ayana Khan (7)	114
Lexie-Mae Darbyshire (10)	72	Ameera Hussain (7)	115
Atharva Chandan (10)	73	Noraiz Ashraf (10)	116
Corey Graham (10)	74	Inaya Hussain (9)	117
Christian Rembowski (10)	75	Zayaan Khan (7)	118
Lee Stewart (10)	76	Raees Ali (7)	119
Benji Morrow (10)	77	Cassie Andrade (10)	120
Maisy May Taylor (11)	78	Shellyann Djambi (7)	121
Jasmine Morgans (10)	79	Naomi Sieranska (9)	122
Olan Tely (11)	80	Anaya Khan (7)	123
Isabella Double (10)	81	Haniyah Sheikh (8)	124
Eliza Taylor (11)	82	Muhammad Sattar (7)	125
Isla Didd (10)	83	Yara Abrkias (10)	126
Leo Houlston (10)	84	Husnain Amer (7)	127
Scarlett Bowler (11)	85	Maryam Farukh (7)	128
Hayden Whyte (11)	86	Hafsa Islam (7)	129
Sam Antrobus (10)	87	Dua (7)	130
Marcel Szaldeski (10)	88	Kaif Hussain (9)	131
Kayla Mai (10)	89	Kiran Ombang (7)	132
Michalina Wisniewska (11)	90	Jayden Ichull (7)	133
Ralph Cesar (10)	91	Safa Hussain (7)	134
		Anaayah Ali (7)	135

St Michael's CE Primary School, Bolton

Aleeza Ahmed (9)	92	Amaan Hussain (7)	136
Sanah Shafiq (9)	94	Taha Chaudhry (7)	137
Byamungu Asa (9)	96	Jacob Arrandale (8)	138
Aisha Javed (7)	98	Sebastian Brook (7)	139
Ayesha Naveed (8)	99	Idris Qazi (7)	140
Fatima Asim (10)	100	Ayat Hussain (7)	141
		Zakariyah Haider (7)	142
		Haaris Ahmed (7)	143

Mohammad Osman Ullah (7)	144
Dawood Farooq (10)	145
Anum Khan (7)	146
Jannat Habib (9)	147
Furqan Mahmood (9)	148
Mahzala Tiraki (8)	149
Aabro Zara (9)	150
Zoya Ali (9)	151
Aisha Saleem (9)	152
Shayaan Khan (7)	153
Iman Irfan (9)	154
Noman Farooq (7)	155
Danial Baig (9)	156

St Stephen's School & Children's Centre, London

Muhammad Tosif Patel (9)	157
Maryam Patel (9)	158
Sabit Chowdhury (9)	159
Maryam Ali (10)	160
Safwana Khan (10)	161
Tawfiq Khalifa (10)	162
Aiyzah Rasool (9)	163
Vedant Dhakecha (9)	164
Samuel Chapman (9)	165
Ayaan Azaan Mohammad (9)	166
Yahya Uddin (9)	167
Saniha Samreen (9)	168
Samah Ali (9)	169
Maidah Farooq (9)	170
Ramisa Amin (9)	171
Jai Vijay Patel (9)	172
Shreya Vishnu (9)	173
Mahmudur Rahaman (9)	174
Fatima Aqeel (9)	175
Naitri Prajapati (9)	176

Trinity All Saints CE Primary School, Bingley

Amelia Mason (9)	177
Laiba Ali (9)	178
Amelia Farooqi (9)	179
Hannah Brown (10)	180
Megan Wood (9)	181
Angelica Hardy (9)	182
Daisy Mort (9)	183
Zaynah Rashid (9)	184
Hareem Haroon (9)	185
Quinn Carrintton	186
Jack Mason (9)	187
Aleena Ahmed (10)	188
Aiza Masud (9)	189
Thomas Eden (9)	190
Stanley Batters (10)	191
Erin Irwin (9)	192
Nicole Hey (9)	193
Iris Rubery (9)	194
Jack McEvoy Innes (9)	195
Saanvika Kunapuram (10)	196

THE POEMS

My Marvellous Dogs

My marvellous dogs, big and cute,
Could they be wearing a beautiful suit?
They are nurses, why would I want more,
On a walk, they love to explore.
They love watching cows, very loyal
And they love burying bones in the soil.
They are cute and always ready,
They have lots of fur, as soft as a teddy!
Woof! Lick! The friendliest dogs ever,
While in their weight they are as light as a feather.
They are my marvellous dogs
And they love to go for jogs.

Zak Sanerivi (9)
Appleton Wiske CP School, Appleton Wiske

My Bunny, Cookie

M iniature bunny
Y um! She loves her food

B rown and soft
U p and down her ramp
N ibbling on carrots
N ot my finger
Y ou make me so happy

C urled up in a small ball
O ver the moon to see me
O verloaded with cuteness
K ind and soft
I love my bunny cookie
E ars as soft as a pillow.

Grace Bell (9)
Appleton Wiske CP School, Appleton Wiske

My Favourite Animal!

A creature of desert and sand,
If it doesn't get food it starts to demand,
Colours, cream and a hint of peach,
Its fur is all sandy like it's been to the beach,
Water isn't needed to survive,
But be careful, when it catches prey it'll dive,
This animal comes out at night,
Be warned this creature could give you a fright!
What is it?

Answer: A fennec fox.

Beatrix Dyke (11)
Appleton Wiske CP School, Appleton Wiske

My Favourite Animal

As brown as wrecked wood.
It is as tall as a skyscraper.
Its body is as spotty as a Dalmatian.
Tongue as black as soot.
Long legs as tall as trees.
Loves eating leaves.
Brown and yellow with a hint of black.
Has big fluffy ears.
It lives about twenty-five years.
What is it?

Answer: A giraffe.

Annabelle Race (9)
Appleton Wiske CP School, Appleton Wiske

This Is Me

T his is me, Dylan, I love football
H ungry all the time
I love all my friends and family
S uper goal scorer

I love tasty food and drinks
S uper good at maths

M ostly I love football
E very day I play like Mbappé.

Dylan Bateson (8)
Appleton Wiske CP School, Appleton Wiske

This Is Me

T all like a tree
H obby is climbing
I love hash browns
S uper friend

I love playing outside on the swing
S niffing around the garden

M cDonald's, I love McDonald's
E ating lasagne and hash browns.

Bella Sygrove (7)
Appleton Wiske CP School, Appleton Wiske

My Favourite Sport

I love to dance.
I love to glide.
I love to stick my leg up high.
I love to balance like a ballerina.
I love to stretch just so I don't end up in a big mess
Because I am as bright as a shining star.
What sport am I?

Answer: Gymnastics.

Maddy Turner (8)
Appleton Wiske CP School, Appleton Wiske

Football

F ootball is my favourite sport
O n Sunday I play matches
O n Friday I do practice
T ricks are my style
B ouncing the ball when I've kicked it
A match I won
L ong-life football fan
L ife is football.

William Ferrie (8)
Appleton Wiske CP School, Appleton Wiske

Basketball

N oah loves to play basketball and other sports
O range orangutans are my favourite animal
A s tall as a giraffe and as fast as a cheetah
H ot days are good for an ice lolly which is the colour of a cloudy blue sky and a summer scarlet sun.

Noah Saye (9)
Appleton Wiske CP School, Appleton Wiske

This Is Me!
A kennings poem

I am...
Very keen
Energetic queen
Deep sleeper
Pet keeper
Sweet and sour
Girl power!
Good reader
Chocolate eater
Fast runner
Summer lover
Fantastic gamer
Animal tamer
Extra funny
When sunny!

Lily Easby (10)
Appleton Wiske CP School, Appleton Wiske

My Favourite Animal

It has big antlers
And a beautifully warm fluffy coat.
It lives in Northern Canada.
It eats grass.
It is as loud as a jumbo jet
And as strong as a superhero.

Barney Rickard (7)
Appleton Wiske CP School, Appleton Wiske

My Favourite Pet

She is small like a stool.
She is long like a sausage.
She is kind like a person.
She is very trained.
She is a sausage dog.
Her name is Filly.

Arthur Turner (7)
Appleton Wiske CP School, Appleton Wiske

How To Make Me

You will need:
10lb of happiness
4lb of socialisation
1 book-filled bedroom
A hot ham and pineapple pizza
A sprinkle of mischief
A pinch of talent.

Now you need to:
Add your 10lb of happiness.
Mix in the book-filled bedroom (this may take hours).
Then, stir roughly and add your ham and pineapple pizza.
Next, add a generous pinch of talent and 4lb of socialisation.
Spread the mix neatly over a tray of baking paper, then cook until fun-filled bubbles can be seen.
Sprinkle on the mischief and leave to cool.
This is me.

Olivia Hyland (10)
Ennerdale CE Primary School, Ennerdale Bridge

What Am I?

I am a sister and I am a daughter.
I am a fish owner and he likes the water.
I am a gymnast and I hope I am loved.
I always try to go over and above.
I like to write poems like this one indeed.
I also like to farm and give the chickens their feed.
I'd like to work for NASA and be a space engineer.
I will do it because I have no fear.
I'd like to own my own restaurant and there I'll cook,
Following the recipes from my own cookbook!
So now you know all about me,
Next time you see me in a space shuttle I'll be.

Rose Christie (10)
Ennerdale CE Primary School, Ennerdale Bridge

My Recipe

To create me, you will need:
A super messy bedroom
A slice of Nutella toast
10lb of happiness
A pinch of intelligence
A dash of creativity
A sprinkle of joy

Now you need to:
Mix 10lb of happiness
Sprinkle in a super messy bedroom
Stir roughly while adding a slice of Nutella toast.
Next, add a pinch of intelligence and a dash of creativity.
Spread the mix neatly over a baking tray.
Cook until glazed and fun-filled bubbles can be seen.
Sprinkle on joy and leave it to cool down.
This is me!

Adara Park (10)
Ennerdale CE Primary School, Ennerdale Bridge

How To Bake Me

What you need:
1 messy room
A pack of Oreos
A pair of nunchucks
10lb of fun and happiness
5 friends.

Method:
Into the pan goes 1 messy room.
Stir in 10lb of fun and happiness.
Stir roughly while adding your Oreos and friends.
When smooth, pour half the mix in the tray,
Add nunchucks and pour the other half in.
Pop in the oven.
While it bakes go to Razzamatazz.
By the time you get back, it should be done.

Charlotte Messenger (10)
Ennerdale CE Primary School, Ennerdale Bridge

This Is Me!

Gentle, kind,
Clever mind,
Geography is my superpower,
I'm not a big fan of sour.

I love to ride,
I jump, I glide,
I tie the knots,
One horse has spots.

Sometimes I cry,
I'm not that shy,
Sometimes I'm a bit quiet,
But sometimes I cause a riot.

When days are good,
I love a hug,
I'm not a fan of pugs
And I love to be a bed bug.

Iris Benn (10)
Ennerdale CE Primary School, Ennerdale Bridge

What I Love

I love singing
But I do not like swimming.

I write songs
And sing them all day long.

I am a singing superstar
And I hope I will go far.

One day I will sing by myself
And some of my albums will go on the shelf.

Some of my songs will go in the bin
Because they are mostly grim.

My family are the best,
They keep me going even though I am at rest.

Luke Walker (10)
Ennerdale CE Primary School, Ennerdale Bridge

Something You Don't Know About Me

I am friendly but not mean.
No one doesn't know my name.
People call me Tilly
But I'm not that silly.
I'm a farm-loving girl
Without any curls.
I love being with my dog
Even though she sleeps like a log.
My friends are always there,
We show each other we care.
We all have a difference.
No one deserves to be bullied.
Just be you,
I'm good at being me.

Matilda Young (9)
Ennerdale CE Primary School, Ennerdale Bridge

This Is Me!

I love Mum and Dad
Even though sometimes I am bad.
I have a sister
But not a mister.
I want two horses
But I need more courses.
I like my friends
Even though they drive me round the bends.
I love watching Harry Potter
As he is getting hotter.
I love drawing faces
As I do my laces.
I love my home
Even though we need a loan.
I am Emilia Johns!

Emilia Johns (10)
Ennerdale CE Primary School, Ennerdale Bridge

Making Me

To create me you will need:
A gluten-free cookie,
9 Lego bricks,
An apple of curiosity,
A pinch of fun,
A sprinkle of wilderness.

Now you need to:
Add 9 Lego bricks,
Drop a sprinkle of wilderness,
Add the apple of curiosity,
Then finally add a pinch of fun,
Spin for 30 minutes in the microwave.

Artie Sisson (9)
Ennerdale CE Primary School, Ennerdale Bridge

About Me
A kennings poem

I am a...
Dog lover
Awesome runner
Nunchuck swinger
Karate kicker
Firework admirer
Gerbil follower
Secret keeper
Craft maker
Winter worshipper
Ice cream eater
Boba drinker
Argument sorter
Puzzle fixer
Music listener
Friendship builder
And finally...
Book reader!

Nieve Fye
Ennerdale CE Primary School, Ennerdale Bridge

My Talents

I am as fast as a lightning bolt.
I am as kind as God.
I like to try hard with all my talents.
I love to play cricket but bowling is the best.
I go on my skateboard, practising tricks.
I hope I go far just like a superstar.
One more thing, I just want to say,
This is me!

Joshua Tandy (9)
Ennerdale CE Primary School, Ennerdale Bridge

Me
A kennings poem

I am a...
Book reader
Karate killer
Tree hugger
Music listener
Nunchuck thrower
Curious learner
Firework fizzer
Winter wonderer
Food gobbler
Animal lover
Cool cooker
Quick grower
Lego creator
And finally...
I am wild!

Max Ridehalgh (9)
Ennerdale CE Primary School, Ennerdale Bridge

All About Me
A kennings poem

I am a...
Pangolin lover
Fossil hunter
Book reader
Forest walker
Scorpion wanter
Ball catcher
History learner
Summer lover
Carrot grower
And finally...
A butterfly spotter.

Dylan Richardson (8)
Ennerdale CE Primary School, Ennerdale Bridge

This Is Me!
A kennings poem

I am a...
Horse rider
Spaniel admirer
Rabbit feeder
Horse dreamer
Chocolate eater
Food liker
Animal lover
Chicken nugget eater
Strawberry eater
And finally...
An art lover!

Arabella Carr (8)
Ennerdale CE Primary School, Ennerdale Bridge

My Life!
A kennings poem

I am a...
Horse rider
Chip eater
Cat lover
Shoe fastener
Hair fiddler
Cake maker
Clock watcher
Schleich collector
Number counter
And finally...
A game player!

Emmeline Ditchburn (8)
Ennerdale CE Primary School, Ennerdale Bridge

This Is Me!
A kennings poem

I am a...
Deep sleeper
Phone player
Music listener
Xbox watcher
Dog walker
Ball thrower
Noise maker
Family lover
Pizza eater
And finally...
A maths solver.

Ollie Walker (8)
Ennerdale CE Primary School, Ennerdale Bridge

This Is Me
A kennings poem

I am a...
Mountain climber
Tap dancer
Stage performer
Card maker
Paddle boarder
Car lover
Roast chicken eater
Brother watcher
And finally...
I am fantastic.

Eva Steel (9)
Ennerdale CE Primary School, Ennerdale Bridge

What I Like To Do
A kennings poem

I am a...
Chicken nugget eater
Summer wisher
Dance performer
Country runner
Light sleeper
Pet stroker
Book reader
And finally...
A guinea pig owner!

Gabriella Johns (8)
Ennerdale CE Primary School, Ennerdale Bridge

I Am A...
A kennings poem

I am a...
Switch player
Mac and cheese lover
Good swimmer
Football player
Dog lover
Cat hater
TV lover
Good reader
And finally...
Cake eater.

Zac Messenger (7)
Ennerdale CE Primary School, Ennerdale Bridge

Dog Lover
A kennings poem

I am a...
Dog lover
Rugby player
Good swimmer
Good drawer
Animal lover
Holiday goer
School lover
Nature lover
And finally...
A science lover.

Bridget Christie (7)
Ennerdale CE Primary School, Ennerdale Bridge

About Me
A kennings poem

I am a...
Pizza eater
Noise maker
Chair climber
Box opener
Early riser
Light sleeper
Dog lover
Animal lover
And finally...
A bookworm.

Chloe Fye (7)
Ennerdale CE Primary School, Ennerdale Bridge

Eleanor Is Special

A kennings poem

I am a...
Snow eater
Basketball winner
Animal lover
Sweetie stealer
Art lover
Game winner
Baby lover
Sandwich eater
Teddy lover.

Eleanor Riley (8)
Ennerdale CE Primary School, Ennerdale Bridge

The Best Goal Keeper In The World

T he best goalkeeper in the world.
H ow do I save a top corner?
I know how to save a top corner.
S o I did a lot of practice.

I know how to save every shot.
S o I won't let in a goal for Wickham Knights.

M y dream is to be world-famous.
E ven winning the World Cup!

Sebastian Henderson-Holmes (8)
Eyke CE Primary School, Woodbridge

Footballer

F riendly at helping others
O rganised as a teacher
O pen-minded as an elephant
T ackling to defend my goal
B rave as a skydiver
A ngry as a lion
L oving as a vet
L aughing with Sebastian
E nergetic as a dog
R unning like a runner.

Dexter Lawrence (8)
Eyke CE Primary School, Woodbridge

Astronaut

A stronauts are clever
S earching through stars
T aking photos for research
R unning on the rocky surface
O ver the bright moon
N o life here
A liens aren't here
U nder the stars, I sit
T aking notice of my life.

Albert Potter (8)
Eyke CE Primary School, Woodbridge

About Me

T hankful because I'm kind
H appy because I'm a good person
I am helping
S pecial because no one is like me

I ndependent and funny
S trong because I practise

M y name is Alice
E xcited for school.

Alice Magill (7)
Eyke CE Primary School, Woodbridge

Spider-Man

S mart as Spider-Man
P layful as a kitten
I ndependent as Seb
D opey as a cat
E nergetic as a windmill
R acy as a horse
-
M ischievous as a monkey
A ctive as a cheetah
N aught as a gorilla.

Cayden Allsopp (7)
Eyke CE Primary School, Woodbridge

This Is Me

T houghtful as an angel
H appy as a flower in the ground
I ndependent as a teacher
S illy as a joker

I nquisitive as a cat
S porty as a racer

M indful as an elephant
E nergetic as a cheetah.

Evie-Rose Mayhew (7)
Eyke CE Primary School, Woodbridge

Me, Me, Me

S mart idea
P layful as Cleo the cat
I nterested in reading
D reamy as a cloud
E nergetic - so much
R unning all day
-
M indful of being good
A mazing at games
N aughty like crazy.

Rafe Fisher (7)
Eyke CE Primary School, Woodbridge

This Is Me

T he world is an unfair place
H appiness can disappear
I f bad things happen
S ave the moments

I n your heart
S o you can remember

M any years later
E motions trickle from my eyes.

Amelie Dorman (8)
Eyke CE Primary School, Woodbridge

My Dream

When I grow up a vet is who I want to be.
Kind and respectful, loving and caring,
These qualities are what make me, me.
I love animals, especially pandas,
They're cute and cuddly and totally bananas!
When I grow up, a vet is who I am going to be.

Georgia Clouting (8)
Eyke CE Primary School, Woodbridge

This Is Me

T he thoughtful friend
H appy as a monkey
I ndependent as an adult
S illy as a clown

I 'm kind as a panda
S trong as an ox

M y favourite food is a roast
E veryone likes me!

Alex Dobing (7)
Eyke CE Primary School, Woodbridge

I Know Nothing

Knowing nothing is my talent,
In maths, I get questions wrong.
My teacher says, "Get on, get on!"
I try and I try
But I never get it right.
Hang on a minute...
I'm really good at English!
Knowing everything is my new talent.

Morris Hambling-Jones (7)
Eyke CE Primary School, Woodbridge

My Hopes And Dreams

When I grow up my dream is to find new places,
I am courageous and brave
Which will help me on my journey.
I want to find new species,
Go to new heights
And take in views,
Exploring is who I am,
I am going to be famous,
Watch out!

Penelope Waites (8)
Eyke CE Primary School, Woodbridge

My Zoo

A nimals are wonderful things
N ature in different places
I n a hole underground, animals are everywhere
M ice and elephants come in every size
A nimals are my favourite thing
L ook at the wonderful creatures!

Ralph Williams (8)
Eyke CE Primary School, Woodbridge

Football Is Great

F ootball is a sport
O bviously, you kick a ball
O r be a coach for football
T ake part
B alls are kicked hard during the game
A lways try your best
L ove the game
L ikes to play.

Lucas Turner (7)
Eyke CE Primary School, Woodbridge

This Is Me

Guess what emotion I am...
I am red with anger,
The rage inside me,
Tears in my eyes,
What could I be?
I've got a giant frog in my throat,
Wait, am I a footballer?
I got kicked in the leg.
Ouch!
I'm upset!

Theodore Burnett (7)
Eyke CE Primary School, Woodbridge

Me, Me, Me

My favourite sport is rugby.
I think I'm very sporty.
I like the running,
I like the scrumming,
I score lots of tries,
I then win the prize.
My favourite sport is rugby,
I think I'm very sporty.

James Ahlschlager (7)
Eyke CE Primary School, Woodbridge

Dancer

A dancer is when you step from side to side,
In ballet, jump as high as a kangaroo,
We balance as well as we can,
Sometimes I fall,
But I always get back up,
A dancer is what I am!

Rose Henderson (7)
Eyke CE Primary School, Woodbridge

I Am A Dancer

A dancer is who I am
Because I am the best dancer in my class.
I do tap, acrobatics and ballet.
A dancer is what I want to be when I'm older,
I can't wait to dance on the stage.

Chloe Fortier (7)
Eyke CE Primary School, Woodbridge

A Day With My Dad

At the start of the day, he is a clump of hair under the covers of his bed,
As he gets ready he grabs a rucksack of crisps and choccy snacks,
In the car, there are dirt marks from last month and a packet of untouched toffees melted and infested,
When we arrive he says, "Do you want some sweets?"
I know his tricks,
He eats all the sweets that I buy,
"Lunchtime!" says Dad,
This is when he gets moody,
So we get lunch and now he's feeling groovy,
We go home and sit on the sofa,
I go to sleep with my Plushie toaster,
As I have my marvellous dream,
I was woken by what sounded like a car horn,
It turns out it was my dad
And that's about a day with my dad.

Ruben Livett (10)
St Elphin's (Fairfield) CE (VA) Primary School, Warrington

Mixed Feelings

Who am I?
I'm a human too, words hurt me just like you,
I don't always feel happy,
I may be smiling
But sometimes it isn't real.
"You should stop being dramatic."
I'm not, I'm trying to express my emotions.
"What do you want me to do?"
Comfort me instead of judging me.
"It was only a couple of words!"
A couple of words that made a huge difference,
"It's not a big deal!"
It is, that's why I'm telling you.
"I'm sorry to hear that, express yourself."
I will, thank you for listening.
"Wanna go somewhere to clear your mind?"
Yes, thank you for caring about me.
"I understand, come to me whenever."
I will, you're my safe place.
Everybody expresses themselves,
Just in different ways,

Make a change,
Help them,
Listen.

Molly Finchett (10)
St Elphin's (Fairfield) CE (VA) Primary School, Warrington

A Recipe For Me Which Only Takes Four Ingredients!

First, gather a cup of tolerance and a sea of silliness,
Stir in some sautéd water balloon fights,
Generously season with failing to do tricks on the trampoline,
Add a pinch of infectious laziness and whatever I hate to do,
Pour in the wackiest universe of unimaginable imagination
And throw into the universal air fryer for 0.7586170 light-years at 10 times the internal temperature of the sun times pi,
Blend in climbing and playing random, addictive games on the PC, riding a bike on air, sleeping for half an eternity, a multiverse of unemployment and a lake of curiosity and anxiety,
Then warm gently by eating half a ton of biscuits.

Nikola Rusev (11)
St Elphin's (Fairfield) CE (VA) Primary School, Warrington

A Recipe For My Sister

First, gather 70% of helpfulness and 80% of funniness,
Stir in a handful of studying and songs,
Season with a dash of confidence, a hint of eating sweet things,
Add a pinch of (peacefulness and quiet) reading a book at night,
Pour in a roomful of honesty,
Add a drizzle of chocolate in, waking up early, the cuisine of swimming, enjoying that moment,
Blend in cleanness, organisation and a whip of playing badminton like you blend a healthy smoothie,
Then warm gently by saying you can have freedom,
Relaxation is all yours and really letting them do it.

Sharvani Kahane (11)
St Elphin's (Fairfield) CE (VA) Primary School, Warrington

A Recipe For Me! (Not Suitable For Vegans)

First of all, gather an LG remote along with 2AA batteries,
Stir until smooth and drizzle in a cup of humour for extra flavour.
Season with 1 or 2 pages from amazing books (recommendation - 'The Dog Who Saved the World'),
Add a pinch of shiny earrings for the look
And pour in a load of embarrassing moments,
Blend kindness, care, friendship and hope,
Toss in a handful of love
And finally, heat with a long well-earned nap.
This recipe makes only 1 human, if 2 are needed you may double the ingredients.
Enjoy!

Favorine Rajasingh (11)
St Elphin's (Fairfield) CE (VA) Primary School, Warrington

A Recipe For My Lily (My Dog)

First, gather sleep and zoomies to start the recipe,
Next, stir in a pot of delicious roast dinner with a side dish of biscuits,
Now it's time to season; season the recipe with an intense running game of fetch,
Add a pinch of cuteness and a little armchair for her to sit on,
Pour in an ocean of playfulness and a sprinkle of strokes,
After that, place a touch of sport into the pot,
Blend in sniffs, hugs, licks and kisses into the pot,
Lastly, warm it by saying, "Walkies to the Maltings."

Harrison O'Keefe (10)
St Elphin's (Fairfield) CE (VA) Primary School, Warrington

A Recipe For Jax!

First, gather cuddles and kisses,
Stir in some walkies and treats (favourite treats, milk teeth),
Season with bum scratches (lots of them(and gases,
Add a pinch of sleeping and barking,
Pour in a lot of loyalty, kisses, tickles, eating and belly rubs,
And whip up some treats, food and of course, toys,
Blend sniffs, kisses, cuddles and playfulness,
Then add his name (Jax) and warm gently by saying, "Treats, walkies," and actually meaning it.

Tilly-Grace Carter (10)
St Elphin's (Fairfield) CE (VA) Primary School, Warrington

A Recipe For My Dad

As big as a bear but gentle like a baby,
His loving, caring personality is all you need,
Treats me every weekend to playing pool with him,
it makes my day,
His amazing food, I could eat it every day,
Watching Liverpool win against Everton, our faces are as big as the world
His cuddles are better every day,
Watching me play football, you should see his face,
I wouldn't be at a pro football club if it wasn't for him.

Harry Stewart (10)
St Elphin's (Fairfield) CE (VA) Primary School, Warrington

My Loving Dog, Max

First, gather his cuddles and kisses,
Then stir in a bottle of craziness with a pot of playfulness,
Season with walks in a lovely forest,
Add a pinch of funniness and tiredness,
Pour in an infinity amount of his toys, his balls
And treats after barking at people,
Blend in lovingness, kindness and lots of barking,
Warm gently with loving his family,
Lastly, put it into the oven with love and wait.

Bethany McAleese (10)
St Elphin's (Fairfield) CE (VA) Primary School, Warrington

A Recipe For My Little Brother

First, gather funny jokes and tug of war,
Stir in a bucket of playfulness and love,
Season with some hide-and-seek,
Add a pinch of cunning and mischievous ideas,
Pour in a jumping ocean of energy and pillow fights
And a mug full of laughter,
Blend excitement, loyalty, confidence and speed as fast as a cheetah,
Then warm gently, by a cup of hot chocolate with an adventurous book.

Prithviraj Chauhan (10)
St Elphin's (Fairfield) CE (VA) Primary School, Warrington

To My Beloved Dog, Coffee

First, gather a handful of playfulness and a thousand handfuls of cuddles,
Stir it with a teaspoon of treats,
After you season it with games of fetch and all his confidence,
Add a pinch of never quiet ever, ever again,
Pour in the meaning of life and all the love in the universe,
Blend in the licks, cuddles, kindness and zooms,
Then warm gently with the close of the caretakers.

Ana Popesu (10)
St Elphin's (Fairfield) CE (VA) Primary School, Warrington

A Recipe For My Dog, Marvin

First, gather lovingness and luxuriousness, along with a cup of trust,
Now stir in some golden hair everywhere,
Season with endless tasty treats,
Add a pinch of tail chasing now and then,
Pour in frantic doggy paddling
And two pints of loyalness and trust,
Blend in braveness, smiling, stubbornness and adorably sleeping,
Then warm gently by napping on laps lazily.

Ivy Valade (10)
St Elphin's (Fairfield) CE (VA) Primary School, Warrington

A Recipe For My Dog, Peggy

First, gather craziness and zoomies,
Stir in an over-full box of flowing toys and treats,
Season with games of go fetch!
Add a pinch of jump-fulness,
Pour in teeth like a shark's!
And wants a belly rub every second!
Blend licks and cuddles and loves her snuggles,
Then warm gently by saying, "Walkies!"
Makes her tail wag like a tornado.

Scarlett Smith (11)
St Elphin's (Fairfield) CE (VA) Primary School, Warrington

A Recipe For My Pet, MIlly

First, gather loyalness and calmness,
Stir in some love and hugs,
Season with adventures and treats,
Add a pinch of sunbathing and attention,
Pour in humans and majesty,
And throw in some heartwarming beauty,
Wonderfulness, braveness, eating and sleeping,
Blend in adorableness and fluffiness,
Then warm gently with care and confidence.

Macie Lea (11)
St Elphin's (Fairfield) CE (VA) Primary School, Warrington

A Recipe For My Dog, George

First, gather a handful of snuggles,
Stir in a pot of tummy rubs and mail to eat,
Season with playfulness and a very hyper dog,
Add a pinch of cuddles, walks and kisses,
Pour in an adventure of jumping into water
And a blend of playing with other dogs,
Whisk hope, kindness, family and bravery,
Then warm gently by adding a woof, woof.

Alexis Hatchman (10)
St Elphin's (Fairfield) CE (VA) Primary School, Warrington

A Recipe For Eddie, My Beloved Dog

First, gather lots of belly rubs and love,
Stir in a mix of walks and cuddles,
Season with sleeping on your lap,
Add a pinch of playing with his toys,
Pour in a soft, calm, loving friend
And a cuddly teddy bear,
Blend a lot of food and a nice warm blanket,
Then warm gently by saying, "Let's go for a ride in the car."

Oscar Burgess (10)
St Elphin's (Fairfield) CE (VA) Primary School, Warrington

A Recipe For Dexter

First, gather a handful of treats,
Pour in a world's worth of kisses and cuddles,
Season with new toys,
Add a pinch of sleeping with teddies,
Blend sniffing and licking,
Serve a good Sunday dinner,
Knead the dough with silliness and kindness,
Decorate with lots of sniffing presents,
Serve with a cup of Mum's tea.

Ellie Brown (11)
St Elphin's (Fairfield) CE (VA) Primary School, Warrington

A Recipe For My Mum

First, gather a teaspoon of love and cake,
Stir in kisses and shake,
Season with cuddles and do it like you mean it,
Add a pinch of hope and it will fit,
Pour in faith, all that you can
And bravery and thought and place it in a pan,
Blend in happiness, joyfulness and fun,
Then warm it all up with patience and you're done!

Luca Harrison (10)
St Elphin's (Fairfield) CE (VA) Primary School, Warrington

My Recipe For Me

Firstly, gather a bucketful of sassiness with a touch of silliness,
Stir in some bright colours with a touch of creativity,
Season with colouring pencils, colouring book points, plenty of drawing skills,
Add a pinch of tiredness,
Then blend in happiness and sassiness,
Then warm gently by giving me a blanket.

Lexie-Mae Darbyshire (10)
St Elphin's (Fairfield) CE (VA) Primary School, Warrington

A Recipe For Nobito

First, gather adventure and gaming,
Stir in a pint of sleeping,
Seasoned with a drop of hockey,
Add a drizzle of laughter.

Add a pinch of Minecraft,
Then pour in a bowl of friendship,
Blend in Roblox
And stares and stars.

Then warm gently,
Give a four-foot chocolate bar.

Atharva Chandan (10)
St Elphin's (Fairfield) CE (VA) Primary School, Warrington

All About Otis

First, gather silly and happy,
Start gathering silly toys,
Stir in his little hands grabbing stuff,
And kicking you while sitting on your lap,
Pour in a bucket of smiles,
And a running toy that he can't catch,
Mix in some laughter,
Finally, stir in some dancing fruit to keep him happy.

Corey Graham (10)
St Elphin's (Fairfield) CE (VA) Primary School, Warrington

A Recipe For My Mum

First, gather a big mouth of potatoes,
Stir in a shelf of long books,
Season with love and kindness,
Add a pinch of going on an adventure,
Pout in a bit of trustworthiness
And a universe's worth of caffeine,
Blend in sleep, play and caffeine,
Then warm gently by drinking... coffee!

Christian Rembowski (10)
St Elphin's (Fairfield) CE (VA) Primary School, Warrington

All About Me, Lee!

First, gather silliness and energy,
Stir in football and rugby,
Season with goalkeeper gloves and boots,
Add a pinch of swimming in the ocean,
Pour in a full world of games
And a bowl of bravery,
Blend in funniness, sleeping and running,
Saying no homework and meaning it!

Lee Stewart (10)
St Elphin's (Fairfield) CE (VA) Primary School, Warrington

A Recipe For Ellie

First, gather playfulness and sleepiness,
Stir in sniffing and licking,
Season with liking Cheddar cheese,
Add a pinch of hiding in with my sister's teddies,
Pour in laziness and crying for food,
Blend in cuddles and snuggles,
Then warm it gently by going on a long walk.

Benji Morrow (10)
St Elphin's (Fairfield) CE (VA) Primary School, Warrington

My Mother

First, gather confidence and kindness,
Stir in some love and loyalty,
Season with cinnamon as sweet as you,
Add a pinch of fun times
And a bundle of joy and happiness,
Blend kindness and joyful surprises,
Then warm gently with joy and hugs,
Serve with hugs and love.

Maisy May Taylor (11)
St Elphin's (Fairfield) CE (VA) Primary School, Warrington

A Recipe For My Dog

First, gather toys and plays,
Stir in a bowl of treats,
Season with family hugs,
Add a pinch of tugs,
Pour in a bunch of loyalty
And a few miles of walkies,
Blend in a wonder's worth of nature, kindness and firmness,
Then warm gently by giving a snuggly blanket.

Jasmine Morgans (10)
St Elphin's (Fairfield) CE (VA) Primary School, Warrington

Warm Love

First, gather a pinch of love,
Stir in your playful pot of joy,
Pour in 50 grams of pure hate so you feel the pain,
Measure your glass of games,
Now you shall play,
Season with the best of friends,
Don't make it simple, get up from your couch
And have some fun!

Olan Tely (11)
St Elphin's (Fairfield) CE (VA) Primary School, Warrington

A Recipe For My Budgie

Firstly gather funniness and kindness,
Stir in loves and kisses,
Season with a bit of deep sleeping,
Add a bit of cuddles and tickles,
Sprinkle in some loud tweeting,
Add a pinch of games and bell ringing,
Finally, gather grass and seeds and prepare for a mirror selfie.

Isabella Double (10)
St Elphin's (Fairfield) CE (VA) Primary School, Warrington

A Recipe For My Cousin Named Primrose

First, gather nervousness and kindness,
Stir in playing and singing,
Season with friendliness and always smiling,
Add a pinch of grumpiness,
Pour in energetic personality,
And laziness but very brave,
Blend in with some imagination,
Warm gently with watching TV.

Eliza Taylor (11)
St Elphin's (Fairfield) CE (VA) Primary School, Warrington

A Recipe For Rosie

First, go and gather love and smiles,
Stir in her favourite bag of treats,
Season with playing out with me,
Add a pinch of hyper-ness,
Pour my life of belly rubs,
Blend all her treats, sneezes, hope, good girls and her barks,
Then warm gently by waiting at the door.

Isla Didd (10)
St Elphin's (Fairfield) CE (VA) Primary School, Warrington

My Dog

First, gather sleeping and licking,
Stir in a can of food like jelly,
Season with food senses,
Add a pinch of not moving and staying on top of you,
Pour in a jug of deafness
And laziness,
Blend sniffs, licks, cuddles and sleeping,
Then warm gently by chicken.

Leo Houlston (10)
St Elphin's (Fairfield) CE (VA) Primary School, Warrington

A Recipe For Jax

First, gather a wide-eyed stare,
Stir in treats and walks,
Season with toys and games of tug of war,
Add a pinch of puppy eyes and door-licking,
Blend in sniffs, licks, cuddles and walks,
Then warm gently with feeling by saying you want a treat and meaning it.

Scarlett Bowler (11)
St Elphin's (Fairfield) CE (VA) Primary School, Warrington

A Recipe For My Mum

First, gather some friendliness
And stir in some patience and kindness,
Season with some humour and gentleness,
Add in a sprinkle of love,
Then add in a dash of happiness and generousness,
Put in a pinch of respect,
Then finally some supportiveness.

Hayden Whyte (11)
St Elphin's (Fairfield) CE (VA) Primary School, Warrington

A Recipe For My Cat

First, gather loving and caring,
Stir in cat toys and treats,
Season with cat food and sleeping,
Add a pinch of love and milk,
Pour in an extra toy
And laziness and scariness,
Blend in a soft blanket,
Warm gently while watching TV.

Sam Antrobus (10)
St Elphin's (Fairfield) CE (VA) Primary School, Warrington

A Recipe For Myself

First, gather treats,
A good season playing football and fishing,
Add a pinch of kindness,
Pour in a beautiful football goal
And a big mirror carp,
Blend strawberries and blueberries.
Then a nice warm tasty pizza.

Marcel Szaldeski (10)
St Elphin's (Fairfield) CE (VA) Primary School, Warrington

A Recipe About My Sister!

A jar of loyalty,
Gallons of trustworthiness,
A sprinkle of madness,
Jars of annoying,
Pour in a best sister,
Spoonful of love,
A pinch of kindness,
Gallons of a good sister,
Pour in a royal sister.

Kayla Mai (10)
St Elphin's (Fairfield) CE (VA) Primary School, Warrington

A Recipe For My Cat, Elvis

First, gather a devil's hiss,
Stir in a ball of fur,
Season with a cat treat monster,
Add in a box of toys,
Pour in dog energy,
A dash of fighting,
A handful of kisses,
A blend of hugs and love.

Michalina Wisniewska (11)
St Elphin's (Fairfield) CE (VA) Primary School, Warrington

My Recipe

First, gather a bed for sleep,
Stir in back scratches,
Season in with rumba and a hike,
Add an ocean of me,
A bucket of Facebook mums,
Blend a walk for the ducks,
Finish it off with a warm cuddle.

Ralph Cesar (10)
St Elphin's (Fairfield) CE (VA) Primary School, Warrington

This Is Actually Me

A kennings poem

Bunny lover,
Vampire liker,
Fab winner.

Sister wanter,
Minecraft gamer,
Player beater.

Food maker,
Great wisher,
Film watcher.

Wonderful dreamer,
Early waker,
Fang getter.

Teeth wanter,
Trophy getter,
Ever smaller.

Power Rangers watcher,
Hair cutter,
Great swimmer.

Nine older,
Pet wanter,
Animal lover.

Pink liker,
December birthday,
Great believer.

Only girl,
Martial arts learner,
iPad lover,

Roblox player,
Family lover,
Phone user.

Aleeza Ahmed (9)
St Michael's CE Primary School, Bolton

This Is What Makes Me, Me!

A kennings poem

Maths lover,
Sibling annoyer,
Cake eater,
Geography hater.

Game playing,
TV watching,
Super listening,
Kind talking.

Fast runner,
Passionate sleeper,
Tea drinker,
Bad singer.

Loud laughing,
Cookie eating,
Bed loving,
Kind showing.

Sofa hogger,
Mum hugger,
Bed relaxer,
Chocolate muncher.

Bad writing,
Juice drinking,
Sibling slapping,
School disliking.

Sanah Shafiq (9)
St Michael's CE Primary School, Bolton

I Am Me

A kennings poem

Game player,
Ice cream liker,
Fast footballer,
Song singer.

Friends sticking,
Game tigging,
Joke producing,
Roblox loving.

Annoying brother,
Song dancer,
Best friend carer,
Joke laugher.

Friend supporting,
Super chatting,
Great listening,
Helpful sharing.

House carer,
Friendly player,
Helpful helper,
School lover.

Byamungu Asa (9)
St Michael's CE Primary School, Bolton

A Recipe For Aisha

First, gather a playful, friendly girl,
Stir in some generosity and a touch of kindness,
Season with goodness, happiness and a little touch of sparkles,
Add a pinch of loudness and screaming as loud as a siren,
Pour in some presents and toys,
Blend with a drawing after school and doughnuts,
Then warm gently with nice kisses.
This is me.

Aisha Javed (7)
St Michael's CE Primary School, Bolton

A Recipe For Ayesha

First, gather a kind and funny girl,
Stir in some lasagne and a pinch of pizza,
Season with friends, adventures, picnics and parties,
Add a pinch of games,
Pour in the laugh of a really funny person,
Add tickles from my mum!
Blend toast and a sharing pudding,
Then warm gently with a nice cuddle from my dad.
This is me.

Ayesha Naveed (8)
St Michael's CE Primary School, Bolton

This Is The Fabulous Me!

A kennings poem

Fancy writer,
Football tackler,
Ice cream lover,
Mathematics ruler!

Energetic playing,
Water fight winning,
Bad swimming,
Loud talking!

Sibling teaser,
Exploring lover,
Movie watcher,
School hater!

Geography hating,
Maths-Whizz liking,
Sports loving,
Late waking!

Fatima Asim (10)
St Michael's CE Primary School, Bolton

This Is Me
A kennings poem

Dog lover,
Family lover,
Book reader,
Ice cream licker,
Fruit eater,
Water drinker,
Spider hater,
School learner,
Saturday lover,
Outside player,
Maths-Whizz logger,
Animal lover,
Strawberry eater,
Christmas lover,
Roblox player,
Blackpool lover,
Favourite teacher - all of them.

Melissza Puskas (9)
St Michael's CE Primary School, Bolton

A Recipe For Sadie

First, gather a lovely and funny girl,
Stir in some candies and a touch of cuddles,
Season with some toys and being in bed
And a little bit of peace,
Add a pinch of glitter and craziness,
Pour in some pink stones,
Blend with some smiling and maths,
Then warm gently with kindness, cuddles and kisses.
This is me.

Sadie Leigh (7)
St Michael's CE Primary School, Bolton

I Am Me
A kennings poem

Football kicker,
Ice cream licker,
Fast runner,
Nintendo lover.

Sports king,
Amazing swimming,
Maths knowing,
Burger eating.

Stylish wearer,
Sibling fighter,
Computer user,
Confident worker.

Early rising,
School hating,
Tea drinking,
Takeaway eating.

Mohammad Abdan Ullah (9)
St Michael's CE Primary School, Bolton

A Recipe For Zoya

First, gather a brave girl and play with her,
Stir in some yummy, delicious lollies and a touch of kindness,
Season with fun bubbles and Barbie dolls,
Add a little lolly and a pinch of very fun games,
Pour in some beautiful shopping,
Blend with a takeaway and kindness,
Then warm gently in the fire.
This is me!

Zoya Khan (7)
St Michael's CE Primary School, Bolton

A Recipe For Safaa

First, gather a loving and funny girl,
Stir in some friendship and bravery,
Season with friendship, peace and a few sprinkles,
Add a pinch of KFC,
Pour in some fruit juice and happiness,
Add some gymnastics,
Blend sharing and caring together,
Then warm gently by giving me a golden retriever.
This is me!

Safaa Ali (7)
St Michael's CE Primary School, Bolton

A Recipe For Imogen

First, gather a generous and flexible girl,
Stir in some pizza and a pinch of fizzy Coca-Cola,
Season with fun gymnastics, cosy movie nights
And a little gaming,
Pour in some cuddly dogs and fantastic art,
Blend with cool nail art and exciting Roblox,
Then warm gently with cuddles from my family.
This is me!

Imogen Hartley (7)
St Michael's CE Primary School, Bolton

A Recipe For Daisy

First, gather a cuddly and curious girl,
Stir in some squishy mallows and a touch of dogs,
Season with all movies and a little bit of happiness,
Add a pinch of cats,
Pour in some innocence and family,
Blend with friendship and snuggles with my family on the couch,
Then warm gently with blankets.
This is me!

Daisy Hartley (7)
St Michael's CE Primary School, Bolton

Learn About Me!
A kennings poem

Sports lover,
Football kicker,
Game crasher,
World carer.

Clothes shopping,
Cool playing,
Ice cream licking,
Video watching.

Fruit eater,
Sleep winner,
Horror lover,
Annoying brothers.

Family loving,
Good dancing,
Secret keeping,
Comfort keeping.

Narges Malek Zadeh (10)
St Michael's CE Primary School, Bolton

A Recipe For Imaan Asim

First, gather a peaceful and joyful girl,
Stir in some love and a touch of patience,
Season with kindness, sparkles and a little energy,
Add a pinch of helpfulness and a rainbow girl,
Pour in some goodness and being nice,
Blend with a musical and smiley girl,
Then warm gently with swimming.
This is me.

Imaan Asim (7)
St Michael's CE Primary School, Bolton

This Is All About Me!

A kennings poem

Sibling fighter,
English lover,
Roblox player,
Food eater.

Good swimming,
Super sharing,
Good listening,
Bad dribbling.

Loud shouter,
Super carer,
Weekend outer,
Computer player.

Trainer wearing,
School hating,
Mum hugging,
Cousin kissing.

Noor-Fatima Shah (9)
St Michael's CE Primary School, Bolton

This Is Me
A kennings poem

Excellent footballer,
Super runner,
Rugby player,
Super carer.

Fast sprinter,
Real competitor,
Coke drinker,
Water lover.

Super chatter,
Lovely singer,
Taking carer,
Friend carer.

Super caring,
Fortnite loving,
Loves gaming,
Sport loving.

Armaan Khan (9)
St Michael's CE Primary School, Bolton

This Is Me
A kennings poem

Messi lover,
Football player,
Goal scorer,
Game winner.

Ice cream licking,
Game loving,
Football destroying,
Dance loving.

Game lover,
Sports liker,
Animal carer,
Film hater.

Super swimming,
Fortnite loving,
Song singing,
Fast walking.

Mason Alan Barry Hanlon (9)
St Michael's CE Primary School, Bolton

This Is The Fantastic Me

A kennings poem

Football player,
Goal scorer,
Car lover,
Fast runner.

Goal scoring,
Car loving,
Fast running,
Football playing.

Fancy writer,
Fast swimmer,
Best hugger,
Fortnite player.

Computer loving,
Glasses wearing,
Loves playing,
School enjoying.

Raza Mohammed (10)
St Michael's CE Primary School, Bolton

Recipe For Myself

First, gather a kind and happy girl,
Stir in some kindness and a touch of respect,
Season with peace and a little friend,
Add a pinch of chocolate,
Pour in some Pepsi and Fanta,
Add a pump of gymnastics,
Blend with sharing and caring,
Then warm gently by giving me hot chocolate.
This is me.

Ayana Khan (7)
St Michael's CE Primary School, Bolton

A Recipe For Ameera

First, gather a playful and lovely girl,
Stir in some positivity and a touch of kindness,
Season with cleverness and a little noise,
Add a pinch of fun and love,
Pour in some resilience and happiness,
Blend with some goodness and sporty vibes,
Warm gently with my dad's cuddles.
This is me.

Ameera Hussain (7)
St Michael's CE Primary School, Bolton

I Am Me!

A kennings poem

Maths master,
Messi hater,
Great reader,
Awesome drawer.

Fast running,
Good swimming,
Game playing,
Nice dancing.

Bike rider,
Bad defender,
Video typer,
Ice cream liker.

Ronaldo liking,
Football playing,
Ice breaking,
Heart warming.

Noraiz Ashraf (10)
St Michael's CE Primary School, Bolton

This Is Me

A kennings poem

Poem maker,
Cake lover,
Slow swimmer,
Cupcake eater.

Secret keeping,
Bad dancing,
Brownie eating,
Cake baking.

Quiet worker,
Friend maker,
Sibling fighter,
School liker.

Smart working,
Maths liking,
Beautiful writing,
Art loving.

Inaya Hussain (9)
St Michael's CE Primary School, Bolton

A Recipe For Zayaan

First, gather a small tiny boy and my friend,
Stir in some children and a touch of some very hot sauce,
Season with love, peace and joy,
Add a pinch of my friends, Sebastian and Zaki,
Pour some chilli and yummy chicken,
Blend with legs and meatballs,
Then warm gently with toes.
This is me!

Zayaan Khan (7)
St Michael's CE Primary School, Bolton

A Recipe For Raees

First, gather a kind and helpful boy,
Stir in some joy and a touch of friendship,
Season with bravery, excitement and a little self-control,
Add a pinch of pancake,
Pour in some Pepsi,
Blend with chocolate and cheese and onion crisps,
Warm gently with a fun swim with my family.
This is me!

Raees Ali (7)
St Michael's CE Primary School, Bolton

All About Me!
A kennings poem

Book reader,
Dog adorer,
Shop goer,
Red panda lover.

Cat hater,
Sushi eater,
Series watcher,
Roblox gamer.

Nintendo player,
Cake mixer,
Holiday relaxer,
Tea drinker.

Arcade racer,
English writer,
Libra signer.

This is me!

Cassie Andrade (10)
St Michael's CE Primary School, Bolton

A Recipe For Shelly

First, gather a gallon of intelligence and a funny girl,
Stir in some playing piano and a touch of sparkliness,
Season with flexibility, love and a little craziness,
Add a pinch of kindness,
Pour in some milk and cereal,
Blend with drama and dancing,
Then warm with a nice hug.
This is me.

Shellyann Djambi (7)
St Michael's CE Primary School, Bolton

I Am Me
A kennings poem

Cat adorer,
Obby lover,
Roblox player,
Strange singer.

Table loving,
Christmas liking,
Fall Guys playing,
Ice loving.

Snow lover,
Teddy liker,
Ferret adorer,
Chair player.

Duck loving,
Seal adoring,
Ruler playing,
Fish loving.

Naomi Sieranska (9)
St Michael's CE Primary School, Bolton

A Recipe For Anaya

First, gather a gymnastic and kind girl,
Stir in some painting, running and a little patience,
Season with a cheesy pizza, tasty chips and a little Vimto drink,
Add a pinch of energy,
Pour in some smiles like the sun and some reading,
Then warm gently with a cuddle from my dad.
This is me!

Anaya Khan (7)
St Michael's CE Primary School, Bolton

A Recipe For Haniyah

First, gather a bossy and fashionable girl,
Stir in some sass and a touch of class,
Season with craziness, energy and a little sparkle,
Add a pinch of kindness,
Pour in some cookies and cream, doughnuts and games,
Blend with gymnastics,
Then warm gently with a big cuddle.
This is me!

Haniyah Sheikh (8)
St Michael's CE Primary School, Bolton

A Recipe For Muhammad

First, gather a kind and loving boy,
Stir in some joy and respect,
Season with bravery, peace and a little hard work,
Add a pinch of drink,
Pour in some fun and caring,
Add some hugs,
Blend sharing, caring and learning together,
Then warm gently with hot chocolate.
This is me!

Muhammad Sattar (7)
St Michael's CE Primary School, Bolton

I Am Me
A kennings poem

Cat lover,
Good baker,
Book reader,
Great drawer.

Game playing,
Super swimming,
Good running,
Problem solving.

Good dancer,
Nice sharer,
Bird lover,
Winter hater.

Summer loving,
Warm cuddling,
Car caring,
Heart warming.

Yara Abrkias (10)
St Michael's CE Primary School, Bolton

A Recipe For Husnain

First, gather a brave and kind boy,
Stir in some burgers and pinch of family,
Season with games and sleeping
And a pinch of silliness and laziness,
Pour in some smiles, the sun
And a laziness dream,
Blend with dreams and friendship,
Then warm gently with cuddles.
This is me!

Husnain Amer (7)
St Michael's CE Primary School, Bolton

A Recipe For Maryam

First, gather a weird and friendly girl,
Stir in some helpfulness and a touch of love,
Season with a movie and some popcorn,
Add a pinch of sweets,
Pour in some flowers and a hug,
Pour in some pizza,
Blend in some nachos,
Warm gently with clouds and some paper.
This is me.

Maryam Farukh (7)
St Michael's CE Primary School, Bolton

A Recipe For Hafsa

First, gather a playful and peaceful girl,
Stir in some joy and a touch of kindness,
Season with a helpful, smiling little girl,
Add a pinch of happiness,
Pour in some goodness and niceness,
Blend with musicality and reading books,
Then warm gently with swimming.
This is me.

Hafsa Islam (7)
St Michael's CE Primary School, Bolton

A Recipe For Dua

First, gather a gaming girl,
Stir in some make-up and a sprinkle of singing,
Season with dancing, a pinch of walking and beauty,
Pour in a hair and a little bit of bravery,
Warm gently with a soft blanket and some tea to wash it off!
Then add some chocolate biscuits.
This is me.

Dua (7)
St Michael's CE Primary School, Bolton

This Is Me!
A kennings poem

Football player,
Pet dreamer,
Hot tub lover,
English writer,
Farm worker,
Urdu talker,
Tekken gamer,
Bed sleeper,
Movie watcher,
Maths whizzer,
Pen drawer,
Dino researcher,
Book reader,
Cricket runner,
Paper builder,
Climbing liker.

Kaif Hussain (9)
St Michael's CE Primary School, Bolton

A Recipe For Kiran

First, gather a speedy and strong boy,
Stir in some dragons and a touch of flowers,
Season with games and a little dream,
Add a pinch of toys,
Pour in something like a lion's mane,
Blend a wet swim and a delicious pizza,
Then warm gently with a cuddle.
This is me!

Kiran Ombang (7)
St Michael's CE Primary School, Bolton

A Recipe For Jayden

First, gather a dodgeball and noodles boy,
Stir in some loyalty and a touch of noise,
Season with smartness, humour and a little craziness,
Add a pinch of football,
Pour in some kindness and playfulness,
Blend with chicken and TV,
Then warm gently with a goodnight cuddle.

Jayden Ichull (7)
St Michael's CE Primary School, Bolton

A Recipe For Me

First, gather a sporty and brave girl,
Stir in some love and a touch of fun,
Season with kindness, patience and a little laughter,
Add a pinch of drama,
Pour in some energy and flexibility,
Blend with smartness and eagerness,
Then warm gently with joy.
This is me.

Safa Hussain (7)
St Michael's CE Primary School, Bolton

A Recipe For Anaayah

First, gather a super and helpful girl,
Stir in some reading and a touch of football,
Season with fun, maths, a whizz and a little sass,
Add a pinch of cricket,
Pour in some books and maths,
Blend with dodgeball and fun,
Then warm gently with cuteness.
This is me!

Anaayah Ali (7)
St Michael's CE Primary School, Bolton

A Recipe For Amaan

First, gather a brave and smart boy,
Stir in some Roblox and a touch of history,
Season with some cheesy pizza and little non-fiction books,
Pour in some hot chocolate and syrup with sprinkles,
Blend with a nice swim,
Then warm gently with a hug and a kiss.
This is me.

Amaan Hussain (7)
St Michael's CE Primary School, Bolton

A Recipe For Taha

First, gather sports and a food boy,
Stir in some cricket and a touch of sparkles,
Season with a rainbow and a little singing,
Add a pinch of science,
Pour in some dodgeball and juice,
Blend with self-control and joy,
Then warm gently with a cuddle.
This is me.

Taha Chaudhry (7)
St Michael's CE Primary School, Bolton

A Recipe For Jacob

First, gather a joyful and brave boy,
Stir in some dodgeball and a touch of Roblox,
Season with some yummy pizza and a touch of Coca-Cola,
Add a pinch of hugs,
Pour in some English and art,
Blend with love and God,
Then warm gently with my brother.
This is me.

Jacob Arrandale (8)
St Michael's CE Primary School, Bolton

This Is A Recipe For Sebastian

First, gather a kind and sporty boy,
Stir in some football and a touch of Switch,
Season with games, hamsters and a little party,
Add a pinch of books,
Pour in some puddings and joy,
Blend with walks and art,
Then warm gently with a nice cuddle.
This is me.

Sebastian Brook (7)
St Michael's CE Primary School, Bolton

A Recipe For Idris

First, gather a kind, sporty boy,
Stir in some running and a touch of science,
Season with a bit of gaming,
Add a pinch of sword fighting,
Pour in some amazing adventures,
Blend by playing with the cat,
Then warm gently by playing cricket.
This is me!

Idris Qazi (7)
St Michael's CE Primary School, Bolton

A Recipe For Ayat

First, gather a kind and nice girl,
Stir in some love and a touch of kindness,
Season with patience, hugs and a little sparkle,
Add a pinch of reading and loving people,
Pour in some tasty cocoa and a yummy cake,
Blend in playing with my cat.
This is me!

Ayat Hussain (7)
St Michael's CE Primary School, Bolton

A Recipe For Zaki

First, gather a brave and sporty boy,
Stir in some football,
Add a pinch of gaming,
Season by watching a football match and a good book,
Add a pinch of energy,
Pour in a smile,
Blend in a cinema,
Then warm gently with helpfulness.
This is me.

Zakariyah Haider (7)
St Michael's CE Primary School, Bolton

A Recipe For Haaris

First, gather a sporty, high-achieving boy,
Stir in a football and a cheesy pizza,
Season with PE and running,
Add a pinch of energy,
Pour in the laugh of a joke and a tickle,
Blend with going to the cinema,
Warm gently with a blanket.
This is me!

Haaris Ahmed (7)
St Michael's CE Primary School, Bolton

A Recipe For Osman

First, gather a religious and speedy boy,
Stir in some joy and a touch of rugby season with love and a little bit of fun,
Add a pinch of sass,
Pour in some kindness and noise,
Blend with sportiness and jazz,
Then warm gently with games.
This is me!

Mohammad Osman Ullah (7)
St Michael's CE Primary School, Bolton

I Am Me
A kennings poem

Ice cream licker,
Dodgeball dodger,
Game player,
Super reader.

Good swimming,
Cat loving,
Maths king.

Ball kicker,
Movie watcher,
Computer whizzer.

Good writing,
House cleaning,
Quiet sleeping.

Dawood Farooq (10)
St Michael's CE Primary School, Bolton

A Recipe For Anum

First, gather a funny basketball girl,
Stir in some sports and make-up,
Season with kindness, tenderness and mercy,
Add a pinch of happiness,
Put in some fish and chips,
Blend with sand and sea,
Then warm gently.
This is me!

Anum Khan (7)
St Michael's CE Primary School, Bolton

I Am Me
A kennings poem

Good reader,
Friend maker,
Great baker,
Fun player.

Good singing,
Good dancing,
Super working,
Fast running.

Great eater,
Super dresser,
Nice reader,
Fun player.

Fun Jannat!

Jannat Habib (9)
St Michael's CE Primary School, Bolton

This Is All Me
A kennings poem

Shower lover,
Sugary sweet muncher,
Tea maker.

Biscuit taker,
Haircut lover,
Bird keeper.

Dessert baker,
Asda shopper,
Pizza gobbler.

Fancy diner,
Holiday lover,
Exercise runner.

Furqan Mahmood (9)
St Michael's CE Primary School, Bolton

A Recipe For Mahzala

First, gather a caring and loving girl,
Stir in some loving and a touch of smartness,
Season with friendship, happiness and hard work,
Add a pinch of chocolate,
Pour in some apple juice and gymnastics.
This is me.

Mahzala Tiraki (8)
St Michael's CE Primary School, Bolton

I Am Me
A kennings poem

Good reader,
Friend maker,
Great baker,
Fun player.

Good playing,
Cricket playing,
Good singing,
Fast waking.

Beautiful player,
Nice gamer,
Best talker,
Super dresser.

Aabro Zara (9)
St Michael's CE Primary School, Bolton

I Am Me
A kennings poem

Good reader,
Friend maker,
Great baker,
Fun player.

Good playing,
Cricket playing,
Flower planting,
Great eating.

Bad thrower,
Lovely thrower,
Bad writer,
Bad tackler.

Zoya Ali (9)
St Michael's CE Primary School, Bolton

This Is Me
A kennings poem

Good reader,
Friend maker,
Great baker,
Fun player.

Good playing,
Fast walking,
Super swimming,
Cricket player.

Cat fisher,
Home stayer,
Cat player,
My cat is a cutie.

Aisha Saleem (9)
St Michael's CE Primary School, Bolton

A Recipe For Shayaan

First, gather a comfy family and a sporty boy,
Stir in some football and a touch of being funny,
Season with love, joy and a little bit of funniness,
Stir in some chocolate milk and whip,
Warm with a lovely blanket.

Shayaan Khan (7)
St Michael's CE Primary School, Bolton

I Am Me
A kennings poem

Good reader,
Friend maker,
Great baker,
Fun player.

Great player,
Fun player,
Fast runner,
Slow walker.

Good driver,
Car lover,
Weird driver,
Nice singer.

Iman Irfan (9)
St Michael's CE Primary School, Bolton

A Recipe For Me

First, gather a wonderfully mad boy,
Stir in some bubblegum and dodgeball,
Season with happiness,
Blend with excitement and fun,
Add a pint of hugs.
This is me!

Noman Farooq (7)
St Michael's CE Primary School, Bolton

I Am Me
A kennings poem

Good reader,
Great baker,
Bike rider,
Great runner.

Car rider,
Cat player,
Cat lover,
Friend maker.

Danial Baig (9)
St Michael's CE Primary School, Bolton

World Cup Rap

I'm a big fan so come with me
And you'll see the World Cup trophy.

Flying to Qatar in first class,
Arriving at the airport going to my hotel.

I'm in the stadium with Messi and Ronaldo,
Oh, oh, oh.

Ronaldo is the best,
Messi's from the west.

We'll see them all,
So let's play football.

World Cup, World Cup score a bunch of goals,
But don't hit the corner poles.

I'll see you in Qatar
So don't go so very far.

Muhammad Tosif Patel (9)
St Stephen's School & Children's Centre, London

The Story Of My Dream Day

Generous, kind
A super-fast mind
Speedy as the ball goes past.
I watch the ball roll (stop),
Quickly as possible, I chased the ball.

I run, I run, but... I get tripped up,
I get a penalty while the other team fights,
I breathe in and out,
I said, "I'll take it."
If I score this we'll win the cup.
I go back and shoot...
I score!
We went out and bragged about the trophy,
And how awesome it was.
I went to bed and dreamed about my dream play with Ronaldo.

Maryam Patel (9)
St Stephen's School & Children's Centre, London

This Is All About Me

This is me, the youngest child,
At nine years old and my brother at thirteen,
Mathematics is the best,
English is a test,
As funny as I am,
My friends are even funnier,
My dream is to be an engineer,
My sport is swimming,
As you can become a shark
And scare off your friends!
I'm as sneaky as a snake,
Hiding my things
And as sneaky as I am
Doing weird things out of sight,
Here I am, myself writing
As this is me, my poem.

Sabit Chowdhury (9)
St Stephen's School & Children's Centre, London

This Is Me

Rainy days are the best,
Stars in the skies are better to watch,
Me is me and who I want to be,
Most days are good days, then I'll make you smile,
Some days I'm mad but just for a while,
I love to draw and more,
Helping others is my question,
I like to do it without permission,
Pastels are the best,
But my favourite colour is lilac and nothing can change that,
This is me and who I'm meant to be,
This is me!

Maryam Ali (10)
St Stephen's School & Children's Centre, London

My Dummy Cat

D ummy mind
A cute find
N aughty he is
I know he has fleas

T he cat is funny
H e's cunning
E vil but cute

C at, an evil maker in disguise but small
A dummy
T he funny cat.

He is cute,
I'm glad he's not mute.

I miss him,
I'm growing slim.

Safwana Khan (10)
St Stephen's School & Children's Centre, London

Going To My First Ever Football Match

When I was never able to go to a football match,
My dad gave me a good catch,
My dad asked if I wanted to go,
Obviously a yes I said so.
We booked the tickets
And then we printed it,
We went to the station so,
Come on, let's go!
As the floor was kind of snowy,
I just kept on going.
As the team I wanted to win lost,
I was happy with what I got.

Tawfiq Khalifa (10)
St Stephen's School & Children's Centre, London

My Family, The Best Thing In My Life

My favourite thing in life is my family,
Nothing can replace them no matter if it's an expensive car or a flamingo farm,
My dad is hard-working and always makes me laugh,
My mum is amazing and fun,
She never gives up on me even if I don't understand a question or a sum,
My sister tries to help me along the way, even if she has lots to maintain.

Aiyzah Rasool (9)
St Stephen's School & Children's Centre, London

Can You Guess My Name?

V ery big brain, just for today!
E ager to do lots of maths puzzles!
D on't you know, I'll solve 'em first!
A m I funny? You'll find out later!
N ame is maths! Love my baths!
T oday is the day, I finish my poem!

Could you guess my name?
My name is Vedant!

Vedant Dhakecha (9)
St Stephen's School & Children's Centre, London

Football

Football is my name,
But it's also just a game.
You might think it's lame,
But it won't give you pain.

Football gives you power
And I play it for an hour.

Football's coming home
And don't play like a gnome.

So... it's... coming home!

Samuel Chapman (9)
St Stephen's School & Children's Centre, London

Me And My Engineering

Engineering,
Hard-working.
Fixing tech,
On the deck.
Don't worry,
I'm on the lorry
Here to help,
Come check me on Yelp!
Phone's not workin'?
Here, I'm coming!
Busy, busy
Me and my
Engineering.

Ayaan Azaan Mohammad (9)
St Stephen's School & Children's Centre, London

The Day I Was Late For School

I woke up in the morning,
The sun was bright,
The sky was blue,
The wind was fresh, nice and cool,
But I was late for school!
"It's 8am! Argh!
Got to get ready for school!"
I ate and ate, the time was eight!
"Argh! I'm late!"

Yahya Uddin (9)
St Stephen's School & Children's Centre, London

The Park

As soon as the day fell in my mind,
I went to a beautiful park,
All my worries went away,
All my happiness came back,
It was so much fun on the way,
Swinging, sliding and playing too,
Football matches, tennis as well,
Everything I saw, it was a day!

Saniha Samreen (9)
St Stephen's School & Children's Centre, London

Me Is Me

Me is me but what is me?
I could be funny, sad or grumpy.
If I had to choose or pick one I would choose... all!
All my emotions are valid to me you see,
But if I am weird, funny, happy, sad, angry, confused or whatever,
All together combined makes me!

Samah Ali (9)
St Stephen's School & Children's Centre, London

When I Woke Up

As soon as I woke up I went to play,
Even though I was already late.
The sun came out halfway through.
We went to the park to have some fun,
From slides to swings to monkey bars.
Emman, Uzma, Aniya and I had some fun.

Maidah Farooq (9)
St Stephen's School & Children's Centre, London

All About Me!

I'm kind with a mind,
I love to smile,
Leaves I pile,
It's so fun!

I'm the youngest sibling,
Sometimes I do fiddling,
My sister says it's annoying,
But it's not that boring.

Ramisa Amin (9)
St Stephen's School & Children's Centre, London

My Life And Me

My life is the best of them all,
My sister and cousins are that much to me,
My religion is the best of them all,
My family are important to me,
My friend and I will never end.

Jai Vijay Patel (9)
St Stephen's School & Children's Centre, London

Me

I'm the oldest sister,
I'm in Year 5,
I love some maths,
I love to chat,
What a fun day with my best friends!
"Yes! I could be your best friend."

Shreya Vishnu (9)
St Stephen's School & Children's Centre, London

Play And Work Hard

I'm working so hard
In my school jobs,
I go outside to play,
Then suddenly...
I was really joyful about myself
And it has been the best day ever.

Mahmudur Rahaman (9)
St Stephen's School & Children's Centre, London

This Is Me

I am friendly and kind,
I keep everyone in mind.
I am always ready for a challenge no matter what.
Guess what my name is?
My name is Fatima.

Fatima Aqeel (9)
St Stephen's School & Children's Centre, London

I Am Kind

I am kind with a mind,
I love my friends 'cause they care,
I am the middle child
And I go wild most of the time
But I don't mind.

Naitri Prajapati (9)
St Stephen's School & Children's Centre, London

The Recipe To Me

First, gather swimming and friends,
Stir in popcorn, fizziness and Harry Potter makes me happy,
Season with laughter, hugs with family and energy today,
Add a pinch of holiday and sunny weather,
Pour in some baking all day and you'll get chocolate cake,
And I'm fair in board games,
Blend memories, gym and clambering with fruit,
Then warm gently by caring and with hope and nice surprises.

Amelia Mason (9)
Trinity All Saints CE Primary School, Bingley

All About My Sister, Ariana

First, gather hugs and silliness,
Stir in tickles, games, baths, food and prettiness,
Season with a dummy, sleep, cuteness, sweetness and kindness,
Add a pinch of milk, tuna, and trampoline,
Pour in milk, food, parties, annoyingness, trips and eating,
Blend in prettiness, friends, cats and dogs,
Then warm gently with baths, thinking and being lovely!

Laiba Ali (9)
Trinity All Saints CE Primary School, Bingley

How To Bake An Amelia

Firstly, gather sports and gaming,
Stir in bossy, travelling, noisy and basketball,
Season with craziness, writing and reading,
Add a pinch of food, drama and eating,
Pour in stupidity, more food, kindness
And a teaspoon of tiredness and mystery,
Blend fun, history, imagination and science,
Then warm gently with friends, love and writing.

Amelia Farooqi (9)
Trinity All Saints CE Primary School, Bingley

All About My Kitten, Balloo

First, gather sharp claws and sharp teeth,
Stir in a pot of play fighting,
Season with a bit of eating and sleeping,
Add a pinch of cuteness,
Pour in an ocean's worth of loyalty
And playing with his toys,
Blend in a bit of scratching, playing, running and chasing his mouse,
Then warm gently by saying, "Let's play."

Hannah Brown (10)
Trinity All Saints CE Primary School, Bingley

Pumpkin Pup

First, gather blankets and pillows,
Stir in some love and cuteness,
Season with silliness, chubbiness and snuggles,
Add a pinch of laziness, love and giddiness,
Pour in some teddies, food, walks, adventures and licks,
Blend in some games, walks, cuteness and sleepiness,
Then warm gently by silliness and sleepiness.

Megan Wood (9)
Trinity All Saints CE Primary School, Bingley

A Recipe Of Me

First, gather chocolate and cooking,
Stir in a pot of playing out and football,
Season with love and loyalness,
Add a pinch of energy,
Pour in a sink full of sleeping
And a forest full of adventures,
Blend playing with my cat and walks and art,
Then warm gently by having hope and becoming the best I can.

Angelica Hardy (9)
Trinity All Saints CE Primary School, Bingley

My Friendly Cat, Molly

First, gather cuteness and sleepiness,
Stir in a bowl of food and sweetness,
Season with a spoon of toys and kindness,
Add a pinch of loudness and outside,
Pour in playing with her toys
And her love of the back garden,
Blend strokes, toys and oldness,
Then warm gently, my cat loves her food and family.

Daisy Mort (9)
Trinity All Saints CE Primary School, Bingley

Stormy, My Cat

First, gather silliness and naughtiness,
Stir in naps, cuddles, food, playing and treats,
Season with biting, licking and cuteness,
Add a pinch of milk and tuna,
Pour in scratching, food, treats, cuteness and softness,
Blend friends, dogs, cats and outside,
Then warm gently with baths!

Zaynah Rashid (9)
Trinity All Saints CE Primary School, Bingley

A Recipe For Mum

First, gather 100g of kindness and joy,
Stir in the 100g of kindness and joy,
Season with carefulness and funniness,
Add a pinch of hopes,
Pour in confidence, love, helpfulness and tolerance,
Blend in snuggles, cuddles and preciousness,
Then warm gently with gleefulness and happiness.

Hareem Haroon (9)
Trinity All Saints CE Primary School, Bingley

This Is Me

First, gather food and water,
Stir in cuteness, silliness and grubbiness,
Season with fun, cuteness and energy,
Add a pinch of energy and football,
Pour in some love and energy,
Add chilling and energy, water and food,
Blend sniffs and snuggles,
Then warm gently by sleeping.

Quinn Carrintton
Trinity All Saints CE Primary School, Bingley

All About My Sister

First, gather happiness and cuddles,
Stir in an ocean of love,
Season with a bit of food,
Add a pinch of grumpiness,
Pour in a tub of treats
And a little bit of sport,
Blend in kindness, love, cuddles and treats,
Then warm gently by phone, TV and games.

Jack Mason (9)
Trinity All Saints CE Primary School, Bingley

A Recipe For A Pet!

First, gather toys and bravery,
Stir in a big cuddle,
Season with a lot of energy,
Add a pinch of love and memory,
Pour a bag of delicious treats
And let's go outside and play fetch,
Blend licks, kicks, bites and hides,
And loves eating biscuits!

Aleena Ahmed (10)
Trinity All Saints CE Primary School, Bingley

Kindness Is Key

K indness is the best
I s it just a test?
N ow everyone always needs to be kind
D on't be unkind
N ext share kindness...
E njoy the freedom
S o just chill
S hall we be kind? Yes, we all should be!

Aiza Masud (9)
Trinity All Saints CE Primary School, Bingley

This Is Me!

T his is me!
H andful of happiness!
I ntelligent is in me!
S trong as an elephant!

I know the answers all the time!
S peedy as a cheetah!

M onkeys are my favourite!
E ndless fun!

Thomas Eden (9)
Trinity All Saints CE Primary School, Bingley

All About Me

S port is life
T all is the opposite of what I am
A pparently very annoying
N ot very good at maths
L ittle, I'm very little
E ager for the weekend
Y ou're probably better than me at tennis.

Stanley Batters (10)
Trinity All Saints CE Primary School, Bingley

This Is Me!

First, gather movies and food,
Stir in taekwondo and football,
Season with laziness and smartness,
Add a pinch of video games, fizzy drinks and flowers,
Pour in some bottles,
Add clothes, baths and bed,
Blend in the fireplace and Christmas.

Erin Irwin (9)
Trinity All Saints CE Primary School, Bingley

A Recipe About Me

First, gather pudding and food,
Stir in craziness, sass, loyalty, partying and a frontflip,
Season with spiciness and lying down in bed,
A little bit of an idiot,
Add a pinch of drama,
Pour in gymnastics,
Blend in fellowship and kindness.

Nicole Hey (9)
Trinity All Saints CE Primary School, Bingley

My Dog, Maggie!

A spoonful of bad listening,
2 bowls of energy,
Season it with happiness,
A pinch of love,
Pour in sniffles
And a gallon of silliness,
Blend 4 gallons of kindness, softness and cuddles,
Then warm gently by walking with family.

Iris Rubery (9)
Trinity All Saints CE Primary School, Bingley

The Recipe Of My Cat

First, gather sleepy and cute,
Stir in happy and sassy,
Season with food and toys,
Add a pinch of brush,
Blend in the hiss of cats,
Then warm gently with cuddles.

Jack McEvoy Innes (9)
Trinity All Saints CE Primary School, Bingley

Recipe Of Me

First, add in kindness and funniness,
Mix in excitement and games,
Add in art and music,
Mix it all together
And you get me!

Saanvika Kunapuram (10)
Trinity All Saints CE Primary School, Bingley

YOUNG WRITERS INFORMATION

We hope you have enjoyed reading this book – and that you will continue to in the coming years.

If you're the parent or family member of an enthusiastic poet or story writer, do visit our website **www.youngwriters.co.uk/subscribe** and sign up to receive news, competitions, writing challenges and tips, activities and much, much more! There's lots to keep budding writers motivated!

If you would like to order further copies of this book, or any of our other titles, then please give us a call or order via your online account.

Young Writers
Remus House
Coltsfoot Drive
Peterborough
PE2 9BF
(01733) 890066
info@youngwriters.co.uk

Join in the conversation!
Tips, news, giveaways and much more!

YoungWritersUK   **YoungWritersCW**   **youngwriterscw**

Scan me to watch the This Is Me video!